Earning Money

Shelly Buchanan, M.S.Ed.

Consultants

Shelley Scudder
Gifted Education Teacher
Broward County Schools

Caryn Williams, M.S.Ed.
Madison County Schools
Huntsville, AL

Publishing Credits

Dona Herweck Rice, *Editor-in-Chief*

Lee Aucoin, *Creative Director*

Torrey Maloof, *Editor*

Diana Kenney, M.A.Ed., NBCT,
  Associate Education Editor

Marissa Rodriguez, *Designer*

Stephanie Reid, *Photo Editor*

Rachelle Cracchiolo, M.S.Ed., *Publisher*

Image Credits: Cover & p. 1 Getty Images;
pp. 5, 3, 9, 10, 11, 13, 19, 20, 24 Alamy; p. 21
(bottom) Jaden Acosta; pp. 17, 6, 12, 14, 16 Getty
Images; pp. 8, 18 The Granger Collection; All
other images from Shutterstock.

Teacher Created Materials

5301 Oceanus Drive
Huntington Beach, CA 92649-1030
http://www.tcmpub.com

ISBN 978-1-4333-6979-7

Table of Contents

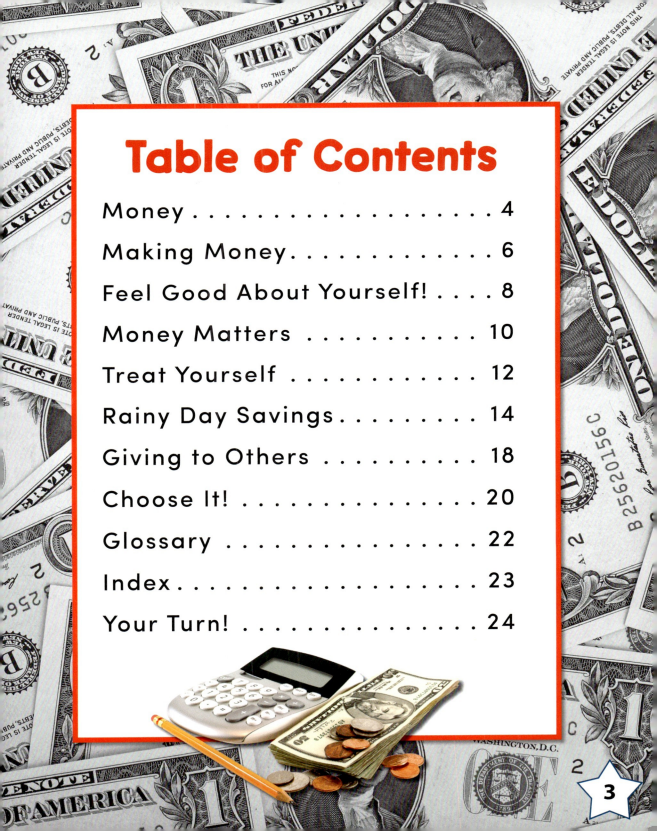

Money

People use money to pay for things. They use it to pay people for their work. Money can be a paper bill or a coin. When you work for your money, you **earn** it.

money

My Chores
1. Clean my room.
2. Take out the trash.
3. Set the table.
4. Do my homework.
5. Feed the dog.
6. Help with laundry.

This boy gets money for doing his chores.

Making Money

There are many fun ways you can earn money. You can start a **business** (BIZ-nis) with a friend. You can wash cars together. Or you can make cookies for a bake sale.

These kids sell lemonade in 1960.

Get the Word Out

Tell your parents when you are ready to start a business. If your parents agree, tell your neighbors, too. This is called **advertising** (AD-ver-tahy-zing).

These kids sell lemonade today.

7

Feel Good About Yourself!

There are jobs you can do that help others. Pet and feed your neighbor's cat. Play games with the baby next door. It is nice to be helpful and earn money, too.

These kids clean shoes in 1950.

8

Make a New Friend

When you take care of someone's pet, you also make a new friend. That is double the fun!

These girls brush a dog today.

Money Matters

What will you do with the money you earn? It is a good idea to make a plan. How much money will you save? How much money will you spend?

A girl and her dad save money.

A boy plans what to do with his money.

Treat Yourself

It is fun to spend money on yourself sometimes. After all, you earned it! Maybe you want to buy a toy, a new shirt, or a book.

This girl buys a toy oven in 1948.

This boy wants to buy toy building bricks today.

Rainy Day Savings

It is smart to save some of the money you earn. Then you will have money when you need it. This is called *saving for a rainy day.*

This girl saves her money.

Piggy Banks

The first piggy banks were made of orange clay. The clay was called *pygg* (pig) *clay*.

This is a piggy bank from long ago.

You can put your money in the bank. Ask your parents to help you open a **savings account**. You can keep a record of how much you save!

These kids put money in their savings accounts long ago.

This girl puts money in her savings account today.

Giving to Others

You can spend your money on others. You can buy gifts for people. You can **donate**, or give, to people in need. Giving to others is a nice way to spend money.

These kids are donating to people in need.

Give Time

You can donate your time to help people, too. You can clean up a local park. You can help a friend study. When you donate your time, you are called a **volunteer** (vol-uhn-TEER).

This girl volunteers to pick up trash.

Choose It!

Think about what you want to be when you grow up. How will you earn money? Tell a friend about the job. Tell your friend why it is the job for you.

This girl wants to be a veterinarian when she grows up.

A veterinarian takes care of animals.

Glossary

advertising—telling people about things they may want to buy

business—the activity of making, buying, or selling things

donate—to give things, money, or time to help people in need

earn—to get money for the work you have done

savings account—a bank account for saving money

volunteer—a person who works without getting paid

Index

Your Turn!

What Can You Do?

This boy earns money for doing chores. Draw a picture of something you can do to earn money.